ABL Bank

DEDICATION

All this dedicated to Mother and People of Pakistan.

Acknowledgement

Pakistan is haven for corporate sector and Allied Bank of Pakistan first choice of customers. Allah all mighty is great who guide me in every step of life and in this semester. My internships are under way. The blessings and lessons of my parents have always been with me and I want to use this time to thank all those who have supported me in this study.

I served in many areas through my internship in Allied Bank of Pakistan. Nonetheless, I mainly worked as a cashier, a customer service manager and an investigator and as a HR officer. Personnel have been very friendly. I am very thankful to Mr Naeem Khalid and Mrs Shazia Zadi both people has help me much during my internship period I have got lot experience where I have learn a lot what is corporate sector and how it works how banking sector works and how microfinance banks works under the instructions of State Bank of Bank of Pakistan.

EXECUTIVE SUMMARY

This internship report is a proof of my working in ABL. I am very thankful to management of this bank for providing opportunity working in this bank. In this internship report, I added brief discussion of functions that are performing at ABL .The Bank is making every effort to meet the up-coming challenges through strategic planning and making the best use of the resources at its command. In this internship report, I shall add the introduction of ABL and their products. This report will include my learning and experience that I got in this bank.

I joined ABL and got good experience. It is slogan of this bank" Aap Kay Dil Mein Hamara Account". It is good news for me that now it is submitting internship report. Thirst of learning is inside us is very important. It gives us chance to learn. This bank is very important for me to learn professional skills.

This internship report has different parts that explain my working experience in this bank. I have added introduction of the bank Introduction of ABL along with the business sector of the bank and bank's future plans is very important in this report. Another topic is Organization's hierarchy chart. It is very important for understanding the organization. This report has also a brief introduction of all departments in which I performed. The Ratio analysis of bank is given in report. The ratios and their formulas along with the Bar charts are performed and give comments about the performance of BANK.

Ratio analysis is also important topics of this report to show the progress of the bank. Future plans and summary of this report is also important. Suggestions and recommendations are important for the management to improve the bank performance.

Table of Contents

Sr. # no	Contents	Page numbers
1.	**Dedication & Acknowledgement**	2
2.	**Executive summary**	3
3.	**Brief Introduction of the organizations**	5
4.	**ORGANIZATIONAL HIERARCHY CHART**	2
5.	**Board of Director & Bank Product Line**	8
6.	**Competitors, Department Human Resource**	10
7.	**Cash Department**	12
8.	**Accounts Department, Remittance Department**	13
9.	**Training program**	14
10.	**CLEARING COLLECTION & REMITTANCE DEPARTMENT**	15
11.	**Critical Analysis**	18
12.	**Management information system**	19
13.	**Conclusion**	24
14.	**Recommendations for Improvement**	25
15.	**Reference & Sources used**	25

Brief Introduction of the organizations

Allied Bank of Pakistan is a one of most beneficial commercial bank of Pakistan. Allied Bank **Head Office:** Plot No. 14, Sector MB, DHA, Phase 6, Lahore with its registered Offices in Karachi and Lahore, is one of the largest banks within the country with over 1150 branches, ATMs and POS Machines at most of shopping centers in Pakistan.

Overview of the Organization

A) Brief History Banking

This Bank was established before independence in 1942 in Lahore with the name Australasia Bank; it becomes the Allied Bank of Pakistan in 1974.

The firm acquired a group including the Ibrahim Group in August 2004 owing to the capital reconstruction; in 2005, this business was renamed Allied Firm Limited.

Currently, the Bank is a pillar with a stable property, cash, and deposits, and its life is over 78 years old. It provides central banking, thus concentrating on retail banking. The Bank has a large network of more than 1150 online branches and ATMs in Pakistan and provides its varied customers various digital products and services.

The success of banking efficiency cannot be judged by using banking and interest rates on their own. Parts of the spread of this increase could be attributed to the costs of the reform process, which would add to banks ' operational costs by disclosing genuine classification of credit quality and provision requirements under strict supervision by the State Bank of Pakistan. But it did make a positive contribution to good health.

While the tax rate on the banking system has been slightly reduced over the past decade, the bank has finally paid huge amounts in the form of advance taxes especially in the public sector. This not only depleted the banks ' after-tax income, but also their future income generation. It has led to greater proliferation and therefore banks alone cannot be held to account for this. This exogenous influence another possible cause of this trend could be aggressive IMF tax revenue targets and the restricted CBR alternative available.

In this regard, banks saw relief towards the end of FY02; the banks earned Rs 220 billion of PIBs from their claims in support of CBR. In the next months, this should enable banks further reduce their distribution.

A recent World Bank study confirms that financial inclusion has a very positive relationship. Further rapid economic development and alleviation of deprivation. In the light of these challenges, Pakistan State Bank aims, in a variety of actions, to address financial exclusion. It also seeks to improve financial services distribution through technology-based branchless banking, virtual wallets, etc. Let me ask what I am speaking about, our progress and the current scenario of financial integration. Core component of the Financial Sector development Strategy is financial inclusion. The plan is to make a financial market a fair system with efficient financial services based on the market, to provide the poor and marginalized population, including women and young people, which is otherwise excluded. The economic intelligence service of Pakistan's 2010 and 2011 economist magazine ranked Pakistan micro-finance regulation in the world No. 1. Pakistan has been transformed into one of the world's fastest growing branchless banking markets. These trends include greater competition, technological innovation, new business models, customer needs and behavioral transformation and the regulatory proportionality. Pakistan is now recognized for its economy and the regulatory climate of branchless banking by international development organizations and media. However, Pakistan is a case in point for how public and private institutions together can push a nation toward a financially sustainable digital system, according to a recent CGAP report. The branchless banking sector would, in reality, long term control the retail banking landscape. Branchless banking has also proven an effective tool in moving government payments to citizens (G 2P) in difficult times such as internal operation. IDPs and flooding over 3 years and Benazir Revenue Support Program users become displaced. This platform shall continue to play an important role in fostering financial inclusion and handling government-to-person (G2P) programs such as wage disbursement, pensions, BISP, Watan Cards, cards and tax collection systems in Pakistan, among others, in the coming days. The current non-industry banking implementations are able to meet the needs of more than 10 million future G2P beneficiaries in Pakistan. DFID also working with the State Bank of Pakistan to introduce the financial inclusion initiative. Agriculture and housing that supports the economy by solving market failures, regulatory barriers and production bottlenecks, and protecting consumers. Lack of financial literacy is a significant constraint in the advance of financial inclusion The State Bank of Pakistan has initiated last year's first national program of financial literacy, which has concluded a pilot phase with approximately 50,000 participants in various provincial and tribal regions with a focus on low-income Families. Soon we will see the impacts of those initiatives, which should provide the marginalized segment of society with more opportunities so that they play a part in the country's development. At this point you are aware that you will have several queries, some of which your mentors will address, others unanswered, and that you must use your imaginations and experience for them. Some of you have already chosen a path and some of you have yet to determine what is more desirable for you, such as. How much more do you know in which organization? Should you be contributing to a rapidly growing private sector? Do you need to apply for a job or study? Do this with the utmost of consideration and determination I am confident that you can accomplish your goals and drive you towards a more prosperous future by way of creative thinking and questioning traditional wisdom.

Again I would like to welcome all students who are graduating today. I wish you good success in your life.

B) ORGANIZATIONAL HIERARCHY CHART

Board of Directors

- Mohammad Naeem Mukhtar (Chairman)
- Muhammad Waseem Mukhtar
- Sheikh Mukhtar Ahmad
- Abdul Aziz Khan
- Zafer Iqbal
- Dr. Muhammad Akram Sheikh
- Nazra Bashir
- Tahir Hassan Qureshi (CEO)

C) BUSINESS VOLUME

Let us explain the business volume

Deposits Rs.805.1 billion (2015: Rs.734.6 billion)	Up by 10%
Loans & Investments Rs.920.1 billion (2015: Rs.865.9 billion)	Up by 6%
Total Assets Rs.1,069.6 billion (2015: Rs.991.7 billion)	Up by 8%
Profit (before provisions) Rs.14.427 billion (2015: Rs.15.120 billion)	-4.5%

EPS (2015: Rs.13.2)   12.6

ROE (2015: 23.3%)   20.3%

D) PRODUCT LINE Personal Banking

- Allied Basic Banking Account
- Current Account
- Allied Youth Account
- Allied Asaan Account
- Allied Express Account
- Allied Rising Star
- Allied Senior Citizen Account
- Foreign Currency Deposits
- Allied Munafa Account

- Behtar Munafa account (BMA)
- Mahana Aamdani Package Allied Bachat Scheme (ABS)
- Allied e-Savers Accounts (ESA)
- Utility bills
- Lockers
- Agriculture finance
- Import Export business/Trade finance
- Allied bank rupee traveller cheques
- Seasonal finance
- On line banking
- Internet banking
- Visa credit card

Allied Saving & Term Deposit

- Allied Term Plus Deposits
- Foreign Currency Term Deposit
- Allied Advance Profit Plus Payment
- Platinum Rewarding Profit Account

Bancassurance

- Alsurance
- Asaan Zindagi Plan

- Virasat Plan
- ILM & Anmol Rishtey
- Allied Accelerated Savings Plan
- Savings and Retirement Plan

Credit & Debit Cards

- Allied Visa Premium Debit Card
- Allied Cash+Shop Visa Debit Card
- Secure Online Shopping (Verified by Visa)
- Allied Visa Credit Card
- Deals and Discounts
- Allied UPI & PayPak Debit Card
- Allied EZCash Prepaid Card

Digital Banking Services

- myABL Digital Banking
- myABL Personal Internet Banking
- myABL FonePay
- goCashless Campaign
- Allied Bank Open Banking
- Biometric ATM Service
- Branch POS Facility

Domestic Remittance

- Jazz Cash
- Pay Anyone

E) COMPETITORS

Bank Al Habib, UBL, HBL, MCB, Bank Al Falah, Faisal Bank, Meezan Bank, Sunehri bank, BOP, & Others.

DEPARTMENTS

Human Resource Planning and Forecasting

Allied Bank of Pakistan the HR process is included on the following different steps:
- Capacity of HR
- Gap Analysis
- HR strategies for organization

1: Capacity of HR

Allied Bank specifically relies on the capacity building of its current human capital. The Bank has founded the training centers in Lahore and Karachi many other cities of the country to accomplish these objectives. Both centers are fantastic and encourage the skills and knowledge of the Bank's employees. The Allied Bank has established the skills of the employees in the training sector which contributes to progress in its work. The Allied Bank also provides its officers with further training, certificates and leisure activities for their proper work.

2: Gap Analysis

The review of the void is a procedure carried out in the Bank to strengthen the Bank's future planning and its current position. Allied Bank of Pakistan conducts an analysis of the market status and its various market competitors. The study of the void is used to prepare the future.

3: HR Strategies for organization.

The Allied Bank of Pakistan is associated with several approaches to carry out various works. The Bank's other strategies need these strategies for its proper work.

These strategies may include the
- Recruitment and selection strategies
- Training and development strategies
- Collaboration strategies
- Outsourcing strategies

Forecasting HR Requirements

The Allied Bank uses the strategic objectives to grow it. The Allied Bank develops its workplace capabilities through some issues.

Methods to Forecast HR needs

The Allied Bank uses the trend analysis approach to predict the HR criteria. It system has been proved successful by using its experience to boost the workers ' standards. This is why this approach was used by the Bank. In Allied Bank, this approach initiates the cycle of recruiting and training personnel in the HRM department.

. Employees Recruitment and Selection

Sources of candidates

- ❖ External Sources

Recruitment agencies, websites of the organization and social media platforms are used in external sources for the organization's purposes.

- ❖ Internal sources:

The most common way is employee referrals which are used as an internal source for recruiting new employees in the organization.

Employee Selection Process

The selection of an employee in the HR department takes place according to three steps. These are the research, questioning and final interview phases.

c. Training and Development

Training Need Assessment

For the advancement of particular organizations, training & assessment is very necessary since it is crucial for the success of the Allied Bank. The Allied Bank has used this strategy to gain knowledge of the sort of preparation its employees need and then has completed their recruitment goal. The Allied Bank evaluated the operational experience, abilities and capabilities of the employee in order to identify certain deficiencies or need areas through this evaluation process. Since hearing about the training purpose, the Allied Bank has tried to gain information about the objectives of this training agency. The evaluation process in the bank however, has been finished.

Employee Development

Allied Bank of Pakistan has organized various training sessions for its workers so that they are aware of new strategies and have acquired the latest skills through training.

d. Performance Management

Setting Performance Standards

Allied Bank has established criteria for managing its employees and has informed all its employees about the setting of the standard of performance. Allied Bank for the purpose of setting performance standards has made these offices / branches complete the goal. When you do your job, the performance of the employee is satisfactory.

Performance Reports

Branch managers and area managers are required to plan and develop their bank's performance reports on the results of their jobs and the workers are given advancement on the basis of this evaluation. The Lahore headquarters needs a performance report from employees of the company from the central sector and is then determined on the promotion of employees.

Employee Compensation and Benefits

Type of Compensation and Benefits

After awareness of benefits provided to every employee of the Allied Bank, the Allies Bank of Pakistan produced a report on compensation and benefits. Among the major benefits is the appointment of those workers. The Allied Bank, according to its specific conditions, provides the fee to the workers. These employees also receive the many incentives from the organization, such as medical facilities, etc.

f. Organizational Career Management

Employee Job Changes

The special feature of Allied Bank of Pakistan is that it controls workers ' employment. It encourages the employee to attend other areas and to develop his / her abilities, and enhance the organization's growth.

Job Changes.

Promotion: Workplace promotions take place at regular rates and according to the aim of the workers. The guidelines motivate workers in one year of their program on the grounds of the success of their goals.

Transfer: Transfer process is the most important process through which an employee can move between branches. There is no difficulty in the transfer procedure in the Allied Bank and the employee is able to easily move from one industry to another.

Cash Department

It provides its users with following facilities:

a) Accept deposits:
If a consumer wants to pay some money into his wallet, it is passed to the proper official, who acknowledges the payment and sends the customer a receipt. The cashier in the long book of the cashier shall enter the sum deposited with the client.

b) Collection of utility bills:
The Bank also offers the facility for collecting electricity, gas and telephones & utility charges. The branches receive bills of services outside banking hours.

Accounts department

The bank's one of the important tasks is to accept public deposits. The following are the bank's forms of deposits:
1. Current accounts.
2. Pls saving accounts.
3. Pls term deposit.
4. Special notice deposit.

Remittance Department

The transfer of funds is one of the major functions of the banking sector following are major services of our bank.
1. Demand draft
2. Telegraphic Transfer
3. Payment order
4. Deposit at call

Clearing Department

If a branch collects cheques from another bank than one payment process, you must send a person to take money for you but this is done through clearing in those cities where there is a State Bank. There is a clearinghouse in Pakistan State Bank. There are two methods for clarity,
• Outward Clearing Register:
• Inward Clearing Register:

A) BRIEF INTRODUCTION OF THE BRANCH WHERE I DID INTERNSHIP

Allied Bank Branch, where u did these internship is located at Quaid E Azam Road Gojra, Where Mr Naeem Khalid is Branch Manager and MRS Shazia Zadi is Assistant Manager Mr Bilal is Relationship Manager and Saeed is serving as a Cash officer.

B) STARTING & ENDING DATES OF INTERNSHIP PROGRAM

ABL bank branch, GOJRA is Quaid E Azam road near Chaman Super Foods & Ice Bar where I have performed my duties from 18-Nov-2019 to 31-Dec-2019.

I also received training in this bank focused on Pakistan's State Bank policies. I've observed all the bank's laws.

C) NAMES OF THE DEPARTMENT WHERE I GOT TRAINING

It's the agency description and my internship period.

Sr. #	Departments	Duration	Dates
1	HR Department	10 Days	18-Nov-2019 to 28-Nov-2019
2	Credit, advance and deposit Department	12 Days	29-Nov-2019 to 10-Dec-2019
3	Accounts & Finance Department	11 Days	11-Dec-2019 to 20-Dec-2019
4	Clearing & Collection Department	11 Days	21-Dec-2019 to 31-Dec-2019

Program Training

REASON FOR SELECTING ABL

ABL's branch is in my town. It's around 15 minutes drive away from my house. I have chose my internship here because there are all the departments that are required for my training, such as HR, accounting and financing, credit and advancements groups, clearing and collection departments. There are good staffs in that branch. At this branch, I will apply for work. I have chosen this Bank to demonstrate more legitimacy with my abilities. My relationships will be strengthened with this internship. You can do work on that bank easily.

DUTIES PERFORMED

I have done various functions in various departments. This bank contains a lot of offices. I worked out my tasks such as in funds and lending, equity and development classes, clearing and processing units, which my schooling requires.

WORK DONE AT DIFFERENT DEPARTMENT OF ABL

Credit Advances & Deposit Department

The bank's department is important. The bank cannot run its operations without this department. By using these deposits, banks earn profit. One of the sellers ' main tasks is therefore the sale of bank liability products on the market, especially at low cost deposits, such as PLS-SB and CD.

I learnt these skills in this department.

- Total performance and personalized service delivery.
- The use of promotions across various media outlets such as broadcast, digital and other
- Marketing activation initiatives
- Incentives for operations and sales people
- Introducing new incentives for operations and goods
- To maintain personal relationship with current and prospective customers

2-ACCOUNTS & FINANCE DEPARTMENT

ACCOUNT OPENING

The banks attach great importance to this department. ABL began campaigning to open this bank's new accounts.
Allied Bank is opening different accounts styles. The records are

Current Account

The minimum current account amount is Rs-10,000 created. In the case of a current account the bank does not pay any money reward. Your bank's fund is payable upon request without any withdrawal limits. This page can be used directly.

Partnership

This form/type of account is available for a company that works together with many collaborators. When opening the partnership account, care must be taken to obtain the partnership documents and their special accounting instructions.

CLEARING COLLECTION & REMITTANCE DEPARTMENT

Because I knew a great deal from the bank other section, I studied other fundamentals and techniques on money transfer in the transfer sector, either from outside or overseas.

The transition function includes mobilizing capital from place to place. The payment department offers only its facilities for money generation in the station and manages documentation as well as demand copy, move, rupee and traveler's search.

I study the procedures of the transition team during my internship, which are also mentioned below. In the following devices, the transition department is involved.

- Demand Draft
- Pay Order
- Telegraphic Transfer
- Mail Transfer
- Pay slip
- Rupee Traveler Cheque (RTC)
- Demand Draft (DD)

Learning Experiences

KNOWLEDGE GAINED

The expertise that I have acquired from my research and corporate finance training at the Virtual University of Pakistan is given below:

Credit Policy

In accordance with the lending policies of the State Bank, loan operations shall be conducted. The policy is strictly banned and proposes the financing of self-liquidating, well-supported and well-assumed transactions that are equivalent to the principle of lending (safety, liquidity, dispersal, payments and adequacy).

Capital

It is the fundamental basis, because the money invested by the investor is his trust in the company and it's potential. ABL provides trade and industry with short-term capital, but some borrowers insist that the bank provides them with the bulk of capital needed. Therefore, during lending, the bank should consider that the amount requested in relation to own resources or investments by the borrower is reasonable.

Liquidity

A) It means the ability to reclaim developments in an accident, because all capital spent is reimbursable on demand in a lump sum. The ABL will insure that the loaned funds are not delayed for an unreasonable duration of login and that the creditor must reimburse the whole sum left to them shortly.

SKILLS LEARNED

I have developed my performance through my training to improve my skills typical in the Bank Financial Statements Review course.

Skills to Read & Write Financial Reports

I have expanded my research, writing financial and other papers and company during my training.

Skills to Analyze a Problem & Solving the issues

I have been able to analyze my issues and concerns through my preparation and take corrective measures to address those challenges I have faced.

Skills to Work in All Age Groups

I also improved my ability to work with all ages using my best skills in communication.

Financing, Investing & Operating skills

I increased my funding, investment and operating skills greatly during the course of the training program.

Financial/Ratio Analyses Skills

I learned to analyze the ratio analysis and make quick decisions during my training workshop.

ATTITUED OBSERVED/VALUES GAINED

The habits and principles that I learned in the process of my internship are: operating with sincerity and dignity, dedication and sharing, justice & meritocracy, cooperation and a sense of partnership, humilities & mutual respect, compassion and social responsibility. All these qualities will motivate you to lead and excel.

MOST CHALLENGING TASK PERFORMED

The most difficult task I have undertaken is the role of demand funding facilities and I have achieved so effectively and efficiently.

Demand Finance Facility

The bank on demand provides this facility. It means that the bank pays the full amount to the client and markup is also payable on the full amount. The bank considers the full amount outstanding. The bank provides also facility of loan to its own employees against the security of their immovable property. The rate of mark up on these advances is lesser as compared to the rate of mark up on the other advances.

Critical Analysis

Risk facing by branch

The bank's vulnerability only existed because many consumers assumed that the National Savings Centers paid high interest prices. To achieve great interest certain consumers have switched to the branch, but other services such as free resources can be provided to keep the account with ABL. Although the government-owned saving center charges a high rate, there are not any facilities

.

Risk factor and framework

As I speak about the risk structure, we need to remember that like Meezan bank, it provides solutions for funding on a home-based basis with low interest rates. These considerations could also be planned for the bank and the mechanisms and creative strategies to catch the eye should be set up by the central office to attract consumers not just, but with the bank as well. The same situation is with the division of ABL that the filing system was not working even on the last day of the exercise, because it is always empty in top and one must remove it. Using databases and the automated system could make it better.

Risk faced by the banks

The competition between all commercial banks in the area is to increase the deposits and the number of advances not only in this area, but to expand their business to the rural area close to the bank branch. By field survey and saving centre, micro-finance banks grab the consumers by tag of the nation. This is not a situation in which all commercial banks should meet the time demand and goal given by headquarters by means of much discussion and customer encouragement and discussion.

Security system

In addition to the confidential information for employees and the bank's security system, top priority is also given. There is only one guard who said he is adequate and well trained before the cashier counter. Although he may be youngest and educated, the condition is very serious and needs a great deal of protection. The branch should therefore do this and track the guards via video cameras to improve the efficiency of the branch.

For the depository number and things stored in the bank lockers, the worker still wants the security and privacy. This is the explanation for their trust in opening the bank account as I see the workers clearly stated their CNIC number, gender, and father name.

Employee's appreciation and Integrity

When we speak to an organization like my bank branch where I served in ABL Quaid Azam road, Gojra also matter if we are to negotiate development, and to coordinate time dependent groups or incentives for the senior management at the head Office of the ABL. Gojra should also be focusing on this point of focus and coordinated incentive suggestions. It is important for employee satisfaction and that is my theoretical opinion of the division of the bank.

Behavior of dealing and client satisfaction

My question about the department of Allied Bank Ltd the dealing among the client and teller is properly prepared but inside the direction of the move clients must look ahead to lengthy intervals ultimately its miles quite difficult for a capacity client to get the details. Facilities for customer support aren't correct and in the potential company has uncertainty in preparation and opening up account as they notice the talking style and quitting the rhythm of work (leave it on tomorrow) mind set.

There is no reasonable way to provide the consumer or buyer with details. My staff team from the Allied Bank Ltd department loses confidence if the client is accused of a mild disappointment.

Management information system

Modern use of computers

One observation is the use of state-of - the-art data processing systems and high speed Internet packages. This is essential to the goodwill of the bank branch and the capture of staff. All employee personal information should be available within the bank database. Customer data and your account number and balance detail are also included in the MIS. Now that technology has made access to the bank details on the mobile device easier, it also increases hacking opportunities for hackers. There is also the need to maintain an information system and encrypt the data. For personal information, such as mother's name, birth date and card number of the card to access, CNIC expiry date, and the clarification should be sought in order to automatically prevent any fraud.

Systematic risk

Systematic danger is one that consistently impacts the departments to meet the number of accounts we consider deposits and to achieve the goal of growth. These are publicly referred to by the administration as systemic risk.

It urges branch personnel to work better even on the ground to increase public awareness of the residents and the neighboring areas in order to pay money to the bank. Another danger that Allied Bank GmbH provides a small fee for employees, as mentioned above, is that a number of customers move their bank accounts to NSC owing to their high profits. To order to appeal to the customer, the Allied Bank Ltd has to boom the income charges.

Wise banking firms know the value of the client and, because of little excuse, ABL rarely permits its clients or representatives to leave. The head office always has a leading and competitive policy with rules and regulations to increase deposits with the bank and increase advances not only in the model city but also in the area close to Gojra.

Unsystematic risk

Beyond the control of the banking staff implemented by the State Bank or the Government taxes

Or strict policies made for the banks. If the policy is made that on the profit the high ratio of tax would be paid to the treasury of Government of Pakistan. Another example of policy may be the revision of policies and in the favor of customers but not in the favor of the banking business may also comes under the unsystematic risk. The tendency of religious leader to gain the attention of the peoples in a direction that made the mind of people is opposite direction for banks. The interest rate is prohibited as earning and it should be prohibited like these fatwa's could create ambiguity in the mind of the peoples. Competent banking methods don't give emphasis to on variety in number of debts however greater quantity in amount deposits at the same time as in Muslim Commercial Bank Ltd situation department of internship account are extra however depositing are low.

Loaning system

Eligibility for the loan

The customers who satisfy the criteria to receive the loan by the bank are provided with the loan. It is mandatory for an individual to hold an appropriate bank account with the bank for over two years under the terms and conditions of this loan. No loan was received before that from either the same bank or the other bank that saw bankruptcy. Any criminal record in the event of a legal code of conduct. The analyzes of character are also included in the new guidelines for obtaining a loan approved by the bank headquarters. The person serving the government then maintains the bank account over a year, and the salary of the employee is credited to the bank's office. Before the application is forwarded, correct CNICs should be carried out without expiry of the date and approval from the National Database Regulatory Authority.

Nature of the loan product

The bank offers many types of loan products to meet its valuable customers ' various needs. Any customer needs capital for their own personal purposes, much like somebody is willing to build a home. The various types of loan items and terms for each form are common. The conditions are different. The interest rate on personal loans that start at 16% and may differ in one year by a lower value system and in less than 16% in one year.

Submission of documents

Until accepting a bank loan, several documentation are needed. No matter what the product of the loan is, every product has a request for certain documents. A individual should be the owner of the ABL account and his income should be credited to the bank to make personal loan. ABL has a proposal for issuance of the android program for instant payments. Because HBL offers the competitor branch the facility to make a loan on HBL's android application in a matter of seconds, the customer can be credited to the loan. It is a strong point of a competitor entity, and ABL always takes this into consideration of future prospects.

Approval of loan with verification

Reports are sent to the division of the organization for review and acceptance by the headquarters. These are sent. The office can approve or cancel a request for the loan as a competent authority after proper verification. Loan applicant for incorrect records such as misentering of the employment record or the salary number, if the head office is found to have the right to take legal action according to statute and to revoke the loan request.

Loan disbursement after approval

The amount of the loan may be credited to a customer's account after a detailed verification. SBP issues rules and guidelines for issuing the customer's credit products with time to time. Various forms of consumers profit from the ABL's loan items. Customers are drawn by the range of products in the loan region.

A manager of the divisions should be restricted to his responsibilities, and his position as boss is not always in his place of work. The cycle of loan approval often takes so long that the consumer is overwhelmed when accepting the bank loan and is frustrated with the pinnacle of the market.

Risk alleviation approaches

Skilled Head

I am based at the Allied Bank Ltd in my office and I do not have the ability to manage the money organization, the HOD should be more robust to improve its skill throughout the bank's working life and have the same level of interaction as many consumers to increase the oath for protection within the bank's division. Yet X theory will discover Y theory in order to ensure extra ease of faith and actions within the company.

Training program

Training and courses are provided through head office where Mr Muhammad Abid is master trainer and he is responsible for all trainings and Miss Zainnab Assist him in HR department. The preparation and seminars held in the headquarters shall be mandatory for all workers. Daily reporting and review meeting discussions should be held to analyze the progress of work routine and the problems of employees during bank operation. The question could thus be addressed on the spot or the suggestions to the Head Office for compliance could be made. This condition is managed adequately and best in the difficult field of competitiveness for the company bank. This offers staff a great deal of attention and modifies the behavior and protocol.

Abilities for the planning

Most companies still held their employee wallet in the bank branch and some of the audience increasing be seen on the day of payment. Pensioners and other companies often come on those days in order to avoid the hustle and bustle of events by using a proactive risk mitigation method.

I concentrated on filling out cheques by employees for this when I became intern, because most employees couldn't fill the instrument. There are some who first inquire for balance in their wallet, then I write down the number of 10 of the account if crowd is noticed and I immediately move to the general manager's method.

During my experiences at job cycles along with months of pension payments I have not seen the Manger's path green road map, I frankly took a seat around and looking forward to subjects that seem at the same period the workers piss off and do no more coronary heart paintings that, in effect, affect the Bank's efficiency.

SWOT Analysis

Strength of ABL

In this case, service delivery implies that more workers are needed at the time of the crowd or a business. As in Allied BANK LTD's business, we are always striving to provide fresh, happy customer services. It also needs to be taken into consideration in sequence. Most kinds of preparation are given at the expense of the headquarters only to appreciate the workers to catch people and to create a big market number.

NEW FEATURE IN THE APPLICATION OF ANDROID

Allied Bank Ltd Pakistan is more concerned with the security feature when starting the Android application. For this reason and in accordance with SBP instructions, the application still has a limited functionality, but Bank plans to include many on the line services such as the transfer of funds, the intermediate banks or other banks upon application and withdrawal, facility transactions, investment, insurance etc.

MORE ATM STRUCTURE

ATM's framework was improved quickly and efficiently knowledge base system performance and advanced technologies. In the potential ABL's view, the ATM Machines Network will be improved. A modern technology interface including a finger scanner, touch screen and fast operating system module is also a point of view.

Weaknesses of ABL

BRANCHLESS NETWORKING

With new daily updates and new innovative concepts, the age of the technology is going forward in this area. Therefore the future is important for a branchless or web based banking network ABL must need to move forward. Login authentication and consumer monitoring is of paramount importance and is to be seen in the future. ABL should plans to move from traditional paper banking to soft-form digital banking in the coming decade.

SETUP OF CAPTURING NEW AREAS

Due to the very high competitiveness level on the industry, new areas should be the bank's motto. It is important to devise all new strategies for the capturing of the heavy population.

LONGER SERVICES OF BANKING

Since the bank's operation is restricted by Allied BANK Limited, its many facilities and protection standards continue to be kept at a high standard and enable people to reach Allied BANK LTD. It is very common due to broad networks and fast service is also a gain.

Opportunity for ABL

BANKING FOR THE INVESTER

Investor contributions from the bank should be updated as well as the internship division in which I served internally. In a general discussion and meeting on a few of the problems, Mr. Shahid business man said that all this was attributed to the SBP policies or to the headquarters ' policies. Then I felt that the amount of investment and freedom for return rates for consumers should also be adjusted.

BANKING FOR THE CLIENT

There is an opportunity like other banks that offer a facility to purchase domestic products from the bank's fund. ABL should also plan a simple household procurement strategy and the household items required

Threats for ABL

Meezan Bank, Bank Al Habib and other Microfinance banks are big threats for ABL their services for customers for far batter their customer care response is good. The same situation is with the division of ABL that the filing system was not working even on the last day of the exercise, because it is always empty in top and one must remove it. Using databases and the automated system could make it better. The competition between all commercial banks in the area is to increase the deposits and the number of advances not only in Gojra, but to expand their business to the rural area close to the bank branch.

Conclusion

Allied Bank Ltd is developed organization and is its clients across the world over miles of a long-term branch network that extends across the whole country. It now provides its consumers a range of products and services right at the door. Today, we can claim without heeding with the use of digital banking and the advance of technology, that banking is now in every customer's pocket. People in the bank who always try their best but only because of the vast number of customers the inconsistencies which may occur in the operation.

The suggestions and strategies that I learned in the bank are used to recruit workers. I also recommend that a suitable individual should be selected after finishing his study. For example, the bank requires an operational manger, so that applicants are required to work on the same authoritative post line.

For the sake of duty itself, bachelors or fresh applicants should not apply for the role. The Bank acts as a human being and has begun its function as a service provider and handles pensions amongst individuals. The most relevant thing to mention here is that the bank staff or the management would support the pensioners who are in old age.

The internship summary is both the source of information and a way to increase confidence in the business. A person who knows nothing about the bank, including filling in the deposit sheets, will receive help online after reading this article. I did my internship in allied BANK LTD Gojra, as you have been clear. I've done other professional events, such as Basket Ball, I've practiced with the workers of Meezan Bank. After a work of one month, it was full of fun and motivation. It made me both fresh-minded and spiritual.

After the internship report of Allied Bank Ltd was finished, I concluded that there are certainly some good points, if there are certain weak points. Even if it is compared with the other bank that is competing in the same area. Improvements are always needed but, as the report explains, certain points were excellent. Nevertheless, the Allied Bank Ltd needs new forms of promotional operation. It must improve the play with the other banks so that a feeling of trust can be exchanged between the two. While Allied Bank Ltd has a weak, but market competitive investment rate as well as a benefit ratio, it should aim to comply also with the policies of the public sector.

Recommendations

The following are the recommendations based on my work and research during the days of internship in the branch of ABL quaid e azam road Gojra.

- As the settlement period is too big in my mind, the cooperation of the headquarters should be minimized.
- While trainings are given to existing staff, the new staff must be recruited and looked for jobs in the market.
- The delivery of marketing strategies should be coordinated by staff and forwarded to the head office for approval in the form of power point slides.
- With staff such as the cricket game there must be intrinsic incentive. Many underlying factors should also be included in the external motivation.
- The working workers at the bank should have an opportunity for progression on this stage, as the business also wants long-term growth and development.
- Allied Bank Ltd aims to promote and provide opportunities every so often to safeguard the efficiency of tasks.

- The wall painted areas should be displayed over offices as well as pamphlets of the banking services.
- In order to restore the degree of emphasis to a consumer orientation, the Bank will increase the protection level.
- Allied Bank Ltd is preparing the implementation of regular machine base control.
- Allied Bank counters should be strengthened, because consumers can be readily drawn to boost predictability.
- In Smartphone apps Allied Bank must include more protections and the amount of features.
- In the cash area, there were only two guards present, which show a lack of conciseness, and enough security staff.
- The Senior Citizen's Counter, for the goodwill of the bank, should be there.
- Inspection teams should come often to inspect the properties and report inscriptions and post voucher.
- A separate officer or counter can be organized particularly during the crowd for the payment of utility bills.
- There is really no fast way to pay the debt to consumers effectively. It is a future prospect, although it should be applied as soon as possible.

REFERENCES

- Discussion notes and helping material from the bank record books
- Field notes and study material provided by the branch manager
- Bank related audit reports also provide very help for writing
- Annual report submitted by the ABL during the current year
- Resources which may assist in the process like internet and Wikipedia
- Website ABL and sources of files on the www.abl.com.pk

- Monthly publishing journal issued by the ABL

- ABL Newsletter and information provided in the monthly issued booklet

- Website Karachi Stock Exchange (KSE) www.kse.com.pk

- Commercial booklet written by the writer p.detz

- Finance and its management by William schemalders

- Banking as financial need by ackson devart sigol

www.ingramcontent.com/pod-product-compliance
Lightning Source LLC
Chambersburg PA
CBHW051828210526
45473CB00005B/1792